written by
Brandy Thurman

Awaken Your Mind

Copyright © 2010 by Brandy Thurman
All rights reserved.

ISBN 13: 978-0-615-38133-6
Printed in the United States of America

I would like to dedicate this book to my wonderful mother Shirley Hooper, who has always been a great inspiration to me. Her words of wisdom have followed me throughout the years giving me a new perspective about life and people. Mom, you are the wind beneath my wings... love you always.

To my lovely daughter Scarlett Juel, who fills my heart with joy and laughter. Thank you for coming into my life.

To my brothers Michael Hooper and Ryan Bolton, who have been a great influence in my life. Your support and love is greatly appreciated.

To my love Richard, who has been a wonderful partner and friend. I love you.

And

In memory of my father Bill Bolton and step-father Robert Hooper; two men of great intelligence, charm, humor, and wisdom. They taught me so much in life as well as in death...

Table of Contents

Preface

Chapter 1
A New Light 1

Chapter 2
A Birth of Wisdom 13

Chapter 3
Transcending our Thoughts 25

Chapter 4
Sense of Awareness 37

Chapter 5
A Higher Consciousness 47

Chapter 6
Buddha 59

Table of Contents

Chapter 7
Albert Einstein 71

Chapter 8
Joan of Arc 83

Chapter 9
William Shakespeare 93

Chapter 10
Mark Twain 107

Chapter 11
Robert Frost 119

Chapter 12
Mother Teresa 131

Chapter 13
7 Steps to Longevity 143

Preface

Each and every one of us has a purpose and what we say or do matters. Life is unpredictable giving us many challenges to face every day. Whether it be from our job, career, or within our home, we can't always change or predict the outcome; however, we can control how it affects us. Events happen in our lives that we sometimes do not understand why, but I believe things happen for a reason. Each situation leads to another. The outcome may or may not be what you expect, but the final result will be of great worth. We don't have to love everyone, but learn to respect one another. Everyone is unique in their own way and that's what makes us special. There is no wrong or right way of doing something, it's your way.

It is important to make time for yourself and do something you enjoy, whether it is watching a movie, painting, reading, listening to music or coloring. Whatever it may be, do what makes you happy. We all have dreams or hidden talents within us. Listen to your inner voice and you will know your true calling. Those who have children should remember they are the future. It is important to teach, discipline, praise, and love them so they will prosper into wonderful adults and teach their children the same.

When it comes to our health, I believe the body, mind, and spirit should be balanced to achieve total wellness, which will lead to longevity. As for food, we sometimes feel we can not eat certain foods because of weight concerns. I believe the key to maintaining a healthy weight is being active—eating anything you want, but within moderation. Choosing a healthier lifestyle is up to you.

We are given many choices which reflect our experiences. When we learn from our experiences, we become more aware and understand the importance of our actions. Experiences help us learn and grow spiritually. If we do not learn from our experiences, we are only depriving ourselves of a happier and a more gratifying lifestyle.

Creating a world filled with promise and hope will carry on to future generations. We are the forerunners for the next civilization.

Tree of Life

Chapter 1

A New Light

Here lies a time to look at oneself and know the true meaning of life. The journey ahead will not always be easy, but our experiences will make us wiser. We will soon know our value and the beauty of life.

A New Light

Life is bittersweet with camouflage faces and voices that carry. If you seek happiness and truth, love will follow.

Words are Powerful. They affect people in many ways.

Beauty is not always what you see. It may come from within.

It's easy to judge someone, but you will not get the right verdict, unless you've walked in their shoes.

When you think something unfortunate has happened, something better comes from it, meaning everything happens for a reason.

Try to learn from your mistakes. Life will become easier.

A New Light

Teach children about love, respect, and discipline. May they prosper into wonderful adults.

Words carry the tones and thoughts of our mind.

Breathe, relax and make time for yourself!

Jealously is not a good attribute. You will only make yourself unhappy, and who wants to be unhappy.

Everybody has an opinion or advice to give and that's OK. You decide what's best for you and feels right.

Be aware of your actions. The impact could be greater than you think.

A New Light

Respect others, nature, and so on. The world will be a better place.

Live a little, sing a little, dance a little. Your soul will thank you.

Find your passion, for it holds the key to happiness.

Proper communication can limit the amount of problems in relationships and everyday issues.

Don't be so hard on yourself. If things aren't going well or you make a mistake, learn to laugh at yourself. Who's Perfect?

Prayer is powerful! All you have to do is *believe*!

A New Light

The eyes are like a portal to the soul.

～

It's OK if you don't acquire a certain talent or gift. Do what you enjoy and do your best.

～

A true friend is someone who supports you and gives good advice.

Plan A may not work. Always have a plan B.

Listen to your intuition. It is never wrong.

Time is like a journey of moments that exist in our lives, but I'm not sure about the hereafter.

A New Light

Reading a good book is like opening a kaleidoscope of doors.

Listening to music can be such a sweet escape that fills us with emotions of all kinds.

A lot of us have a weakness, but it takes a lot of courage to recognize it and change.

Why racism? We are all of soul, body, and mind.

⌒∾⌒

You are never alone. Look at the birds and trees. Life is all around you.

⌒∾⌒

There is no right or wrong, good or bad religion. It is your beliefs.

Chapter 2

Birth of Wisdom

We must learn to respect one another and to be true to ourselves and others. When there is no authenticity to our nature, our hearts are not open to love and happiness.

Birth of Wisdom

Saving up for that dream vacation is like planting a garden of flowers.

A compliment, smile, or a wave can brighten someone's day.

A person who doesn't use their gift or talent is like a bird that doesn't use its wings.

Why procrastinate? Who needs more stress.

Read a book, magazine, or whatever you desire. Knowledge gives us the power to understand and to recognize what is fact or fiction.

Life may try to wither you like a fruit on a vine. Show strength and courage for your days may be lengthened.

Birth of Wisdom

Limitless are ideas that are given, shared, written or used. A good one will leave a positive result.

You are never a failure if you at least try.

Criticism may leave the other feeling shameful or hurt. It would be wise to think before you speak.

A man who has faith has no room for pessimism.

Abuse whether physical or mental is not healthy. Try to change. It's not to late. Positive forces will help you.

Family should love and respect one another. A bond so strong will always survive.

Birth of Wisdom

Take time to meditate. Healing wonders are at work.

Massage relieves stress, tension, aches, and pains. It is known to increase longevity.

You may not want to exercise everyday, but at least do some sort of activity a day and your heart will say, "Yea!"

Green tea is a powerful antioxidant that cures many ailments and is known to trigger weight loss.

Do not let anyone belittle you. Though someone may have different attributes, no one is better than you.

People are like flowers, for everyone holds a certain beauty, but yet they are different.

Birth of Wisdom

Study hard and try to do well in school. You may not make all A's, but do your best.

Treat animals kindly. Even though they cannot talk like us, they do have feelings.

Do not be afraid of change. There is new growth and great confidence that you will find from within.

Love is the ultimate bliss that conquers the depravity in our hearts.

It is impossible to make everyone happy. What truly is important is what makes *you* happy.

You cannot change the past, but you can change your future.

Birth of Wisdom

Life is full of lessons to be learned, giving us new meaning and understanding.

Work hard, but always make time for yourself.

Why doubt God? Miracles happen every day.

It is important for us to live up to our virtues.
Our virtues are the power of goodness.

It is unhealthy to bottle up your feelings inside.
Let them out... in a positive way.

Criticism is only good when the judgments are beneficial.

Chapter 3

Transcending our Thoughts

The moments in our lives are precious. Nothing should be taken for granted—the food we eat, the air we breathe or the water we drink. Life is a gift. Treasure every day like there is no tomorrow.

Transcending our Thoughts

Love your children; so that they will always remain close to you at heart.

Laughter is good medicine for the body and soul.

Invest or save money whether a little or a lot. You will thank yourself in the end.

One thing women would like from their men is a little romance.

Life is full of problems. Talking about them will not make them go away. Find a solution and act upon it.

Instead of expressing oneself in a negative or violent way, do it through creativity. You would not believe the feeling of satisfaction from it.

Transcending our Thoughts

When a promise is made do what is in your limits to follow through.

Do something fun for yourself every once in awhile. All work and no pleasure is not good. You deserve it!

Peppers are one of the healthiest foods that have powerful antioxidants to cleanse impurities out of the body. The hotter the better!

Organization can tremendously limit the amount of stress in our lives.

Friends come and go, but a true one is a loyal friend.

It takes a strong and courageous person to admit when they are wrong.

Transcending our Thoughts

Open that part deep inside that wants to be kind. Others will begin to notice a radiance about you, a wonderful attraction.

It's nice to help others and be kind at times. The favor returned may be greater than you imagined.

Visualization gives us a higher sense of clarity which is blind to the eyes.

It's OK not to know. Learn and remember. Then you will know.

Life may be hard and cruel at times. Stay focused and strong. Do the best you can.

Everybody has a purpose, whether big or small.

Transcending our Thoughts

Life gives you many signs. Pay attention. It may be a warning.

Believe in the thought of possibility. Your capabilities may be limitless.

Children need discipline. If there is no discipline, they will not respect you.

If you think positive you will attract positive.

Trying to be perfect will only make you miserable. Lower your expectations and you'll be a happier person.

Fennel or Tulsi tea is said to be a cure for anxiety.

Transcending our Thoughts

Listening to classical music such as Mozart will heighten your intellect.

We are given many responsibilities and challenges in life. Have patience and with careful thinking you will achieve greatness.

Cherish special moments in life whether in memory or photograph. May these moments bring joy and happiness.

A wise man listens to his intuition and follows through it.

Life is like a game of cards. You never know what kind of hand you're dealt.

Sometimes children may leave us feeling stressed, but remember that child will one day be an adult and not a child anymore.

Chapter 4

Sense of Awareness

We are all a part of the universe. The whole universe is nothing but energy. We are energy. What we say, do, or think affects others. We are all interconnected with every living and nonliving organism. Understanding the Universal Laws will help create a world of balance and harmony.

Sense of Awareness

Travel the world. The beauty that surrounds us brings feelings of joy and peace.

Dreams are sometimes predictions.

Life can be chaotic at times. Take a moment to contemplate and relax your mind to a state of tranquility.

Stand up for yourself and speak your mind. People will respect you.

A little sacrifice is necessary when it involves something of importance.

Do not hate others. It may leave others feeling a sense of worthlessness.

Sense of Awareness

Materialism makes us feel good and want more. What really matters is who we are and where we are going.

The past reflects who we are today, but tomorrow is another day.

Art is expressed in many different ways–in paintings, music, words, and life. It is the creation of everything.

Child abuse is intolerable. There is a way to discipline children without extreme measures.

Our perception of life is covered with a veil. In the spiritual realm is when we are truly awake.

Have no regrets. You cannot change the past. The future is what counts.

Sense of Awareness

Freedom is the one who has banished their fears, who is in control of oneself, and not bound by the judgments of others.

Sleep is a necessity. The body heals itself when it is at rest.

The Bible is a book one must own. Read, understand, and pray for the words that speak of truth.

Finding peace within yourself will bring you much happiness.

A hug, a kiss, or a show of kindness can brighten someone's day.

It doesn't matter what others say or think of you. What matters is how you feel about yourself.

Sense of Awareness

Stay focused and you will always be in control.

Does the age of a person really matter to know if they're right for you? I think it is important to know their character.

Do not change for other people. Change for yourself.

The ocean is filled with many forms of life. Its endless beauty surrounds us.

Good hygiene may prevent illnesses and diseases.

Nurturing your body in a positive way—physically, mentally, and spiritually—is the secret to longevity.

Sense of Awareness

The world needs peace, love, and hope. The time is now.

⌒∼⌒

Apple Cider vinegar has many health benefits. Also, it is known to increase weight loss.

⌒∼⌒

Malnutrition, dehydration, or lack of sleep will make you feel very drained. These conditions must be balanced in order maintain a healthy and active lifestyle.

Chapter 5

A Higher Consciousness

You may ask, "Does God really exist?" Look around you. Someone created this beautiful world. All you have to do is *believe*! God says, "You will seek me and find me; when you seek me with all your heart, I will be found by you."

When the wind hits your face, you feel it. You know it's there, but you can't see it. You don't always have to see to believe. Ask for a sign. He may show you!

A Higher Consciousness

Do well, live well, be well; you are not invincible.

———

The future is inevitable. The life you live will hold true meaning in the end.

———

Take chances. Life is too short. Our experiences will make us wiser.

We are timeless. Death is not the end, but only the beginning.

Observe others. As you will see, you will learn and then you will know.

Complete silence may leave your mind to a meditative state.

A Higher Consciousness

Flowers brighten up the earth with their beauty, colorful and fragrant giving pleasure to us all.

War is not the answer. First listen, understand, and then compromise.

Try not to worry so much. You cannot change what has been, and the future holds the events yet to come.

Don't be afraid to speak your mind. If you do not, you are not being true to yourself.

The heritage of a person does not define a person. You will know a person by their use of words and actions.

Chaos is all around. Learn to channel out the noise and to focus on the real issues.

A Higher Consciousness

We are the pioneers for future generations.

~

Being destructive is not the answer to a negative situation. Change that destructiveness into constructiveness.

~

Decisions are made through our conscious thoughts, giving us the power to control our actions.

Omega 3 and fish oils have miraculous effects on the body. Some of the benefits are improving brain function, cardiovascular health, less depression, and prevention of various types of cancers.

Life is a quest to learn, love, and to explore.

The mind is a powerful tool. Your thoughts control your actions. Your actions are the fingerprints of your being.

A Higher Consciousness

A lot of gossip may lead to untold truths.

~

Your goal is more reachable when it first begins with a vision.

~

Enjoy your life young as well as old.

Preserve the memories that bring happiness and joy to you.

To think that a higher power does not exist is only an illusion.

Being insecure will only make you miserable and unhappy.

A Higher Consciousness

What may be dull to someone may be interesting to another.

You have infinite capabilities within yourself.

A loyal person is one who is never forgotten.

A lot can be accomplished with a little persistence.

Every man, woman, and child deserves equal respect.

Read, tell, or hear a joke. It's good for the soul.

A Higher Consciousness

Ginkgo Biloba is known to treat a variety of conditions such as memory loss, depression, anxiety, vertigo, strokes, heart disease, and more.

Imagination can create a world of unlimited possibilities.

Life is a journey that gives us choices, lessons, and opportunities. The road we choose is up to us.

Chapter 6

Buddha

Buddha was a spiritual teacher from ancient India who founded Buddhism. He was known as Siddhattha Gotama. Buddha means "awakened one" or "the enlightened one." Early historians dated his lifetime as 563 BCE to 483 BCE. Buddha and his disciples traveled through India spreading the Dharma, his teachings. He encouraged everyone to have compassion for each other, to be happy, and live a peaceful life.

Buddha

What we are today comes from our thoughts of yesterday, and our present thoughts build our life of tomorrow, our life is the creation of our mind.

Holding on to anger is like grasping a hot coal with the intent of throwing it at someone else; you are the one getting burned.

A family is a place where minds come in contact with one another.

Everything changes, nothing remains without change.

We are what we think. All that we are arises with our thoughts. With our thoughts, we make our world.

There is nothing more dreadful than the habit of doubt. Doubt separates people. It is a poison that disintegrates friendships and breaks up pleasant relations. It is a thorn that irritates and hurts; it is a sword that kills.

Buddha

Follow the shining ones, the wise, the awakened, the loving, for they know how to work and to forbear.

The way is not in the sky. The way is in the heart.

All that we are is the result of what we have thought. The mind is everything. What we think, we become.

On life's journey faith is nourishment, virtuous deeds are a shelter, wisdom is the light by day and right mindfulness is the protection by night. If a man lives a pure life, nothing can destroy him.

Health is the greatest gift, contentment the greatest wealth, faithfulness the best relationship.

You will not be punished for your anger, you will be punished by your anger.

Buddha

Those who are free of resentful thoughts surely find peace.

Thousands of candles can be lighted from a single candle, and the light of the candle will not be shortened. Happiness never decreases by being shared.

A jug fills drop by drop.

We are formed and molded by our thoughts. Those whose minds are shaped by selfless thoughts give joy when they speak or act. Joy follows them a like a shadow that never leaves them.

Your work is to discover your work and then with all your heart to give yourself to it.

If a man who enjoys a lesser happiness beholds a greater one, let him leave aside the lesser to gain the greater.

Buddha

There has to be evil so that good can prove its purity above it.

The rule of friendship means there should be mutual sympathy between them, each supplying what the other lacks and trying to benefit the other, always using friendly and sincere words.

Meditation brings wisdom. Lack of meditation brings ignorance. Know well what leads you forward and what holds you back, and choose the path that leads to wisdom.

They are not following dharma who resort to violence to achieve their purpose. But those who lead others to nonviolence means, knowing right and wrong, may be called guardians of the dharma.

Believe nothing, no matter where you read it, or who said it, no matter if I have said it, unless it agrees with your own reason and your own common sense.

Hatred does not cease by hatred, but only by love, this is the eternal rule.

Buddha

A good friend who points out mistakes and imperfections and rebukes evil is to be respected as if he reveals a secret of hidden treasure.

You yourself, as much as anybody in the entire universe, deserve your love and affection.

When one has the feeling of dislike for evil, when one feels tranquil, one finds pleasure in listening to good teachings; when one has these feelings and appreciates them, one is free of fear.

The secret of health for both mind and body is not to mourn for the past, not to worry about the future, or not to anticipate troubles, but to live in the present moment wisely and earnestly.

There is nothing so disobedient as an undisciplined mind, and there is nothing so obedient as a disciplined mind.

Let the wise guard their thoughts, which are difficult to perceive, extremely subtle, and wander at will. Thought which is well guarded is the bearer of happiness.

Chapter 7

Albert Einstein

Albert Einstein, born March 14, 1879 in Germany, was a theoretical physicist. He was known for his special and general theories of relativity and the founding for the first post-Newtonian expansion. He described the connections between matter, energy, space and time. In 1922 Einstein was awarded the 1921 Nobel Prize in Physics. Einstein died on April 18, 1955.

Albert Einstein

Science without religion is lame, religion without science is blind.

If A equals success, then the formula A equals X plus Y and Z, with X being work, Y play, and Z keeping your mouth shut.

Few are those who see with their own eyes and feel with their own hearts.

The true sign of intelligence is not knowledge but imagination.

Imagination is more important than knowledge. For knowledge is limited to all we now know and understand, while imagination embraces the entire world, and all there ever will be to know and understand.

Many times a day I realize how much my own life is built on the labors of my fellowmen, and how earnestly I must exert myself in order to give in return as much as I have received.

Albert Einstein

It is the supreme art of the teacher to awaken joy in creative expression and knowledge.

As far as the laws of mathematics refer to reality, they are not certain, and as far as they are certain, they do not refer to reality.

The ideals which have always shone before me and filled me with the joy of living are goodness, beauty, and truth.

Two things are infinite; the universe and human stupidity; and I'm not sure about the universe.

Only one who devotes himself to a cause with his whole strength and soul can be a true master. For this reason mastery demands all of a person.

Things should be made as simple as possible, but not any simpler.

Albert Einstein

It's not that I'm so smart, it's just that I stay with problems longer.

Many of the things you can count, don't count. Many of the things you can't count, really count.

In a healthy nation there is a kind of dramatic balance between the will of the people and the government, which prevents its degeneration from tyranny.

Formal symbolic representation of qualitative entities is doomed to its rightful place of minor significance in a world where flowers and beautiful women abound.

In matters of truth or justice, there is no difference between large and small problems, for issues concerning the treatment of people are all the same.

Intellectuals solve problems; geniuses prevent them.

Albert Einstein

Science can only ascertain what is, but not what should be, and outside of its domain value judgments of all kinds remain necessary.

Where the world ceases to be the scene of our personal hopes and wishes, where we face it as free beings admiring, asking and observing, there we enter the realm of Art and Science.

In the middle of difficulty lies opportunity.

It is strange to be known so universally and yet to be so lonely.

If men as individuals surrender to the call of their elementary instincts, avoiding pain and seeking satisfaction only for their own selves, the result for them all taken together must be a state of insecurity, of fear, and of promiscuous misery.

The whole of science is nothing more than a refinement of everyday thinking.

Albert Einstein

When you are courting a nice girl an hour seems like a second. When you sit on a red hot cinder a second seems like an hour. That's relativity.

It is a very high goal which, with our weak powers, we can reach only very inadequately, but which gives a sure foundation to our aspirations and valuations.

He who can no longer pause to wonder and stand rapt in awe is as good as dead; his eyes are closed.

We are all ruled in what we do by impulses; and these impulses are so organized that our actions in general serve for our self preservation and that of the race.

Nothing that I can do will change the structure of the universe. But maybe, by raising my voice I can help the greatest of all causes, goodwill among men and peace on earth.

Each of us is here for a brief sojourn; for what purpose he knows not, though he senses it. But without deeper reflection one knows from daily life that one exists for other people.

Chapter 8

Joan of Arc

Joan of Arc, born on January 6, 1412, is a national heroine of France and a saint of the Roman Catholic Church. Joan of Arc, a peasant girl born in France, believed that she had visions from God that told her to recover her homeland from English domination late in the Hundred Years' War. She was responsible for the coronation of Charles VII. In May 1431 Joan of Arc was charged with heresy, having three major indictments. Among the indictments were the use of magic, acting improperly as a woman in church such as dressing like a boy and fighting in the war, and not submitting herself to the judgment of Church Militant, or to that of living men, but to God alone. When she was nineteen, she was burned at the stake in the Old Market Place of Rouen near the Church of Saint-Sauveur. Joan of Arc died on May 30, 1431.

I am not afraid; I was born to do this.

I would rather die than do something which I know to be a sin, or to be against God's will.

I was in my thirteenth year when I heard a voice from God to help me govern my conduct. And the first time I was very much afraid.

Joan of Arc

One life is all we have and we live it as we believe in living it. But to sacrifice what you are and to live without belief, that is a fate more terrible than dying.

It is true I wished to escape; and so I wish still; is not this lawful for all prisoners?

Get up tomorrow early in the morning, and earlier than you did today, and do the best that you can. Always stay near me, for tomorrow I will have much to do and more than I ever had, and tomorrow blood will leave my body above the breast.

You say that you are my judge; I do not know if you are; but take good heed not to judge me ill, because you would put yourself in great peril.

Children say that people are hung sometimes for speaking the truth.

Of the love or hatred God has for the English, I know nothing, but I do know that they will all be thrown out of France, except those who die there.

Joan of Arc

Since God had commanded it, it was necessary that I do it. Since God commanded it, even if I had a hundred fathers and mothers, even if I had been a King's daughter, I would have gone nevertheless.

If I am not, may God put me there; and if I am, may God so keep me.

Hold the cross high so I may see it through the flames!

I do not accept such a prohibition, if ever I do escape, no one shall reproach me with having broken or violated my faith, not having given my word to any one, whosoever it may be.

Most sweet lord, in honor of your Holy Passion, I implore You, if You love me, to instruct me in what I am to say to these churchmen. As regards to my clothes, I fully understand the order by which I accepted them, but I do not know how I am to set them aside. In this, may it please You to teach me.

Act, and God will act.

Joan of Arc

Everything I have said or done is in the hands of God. I commit myself to him! I certify to you that I would do or say nothing against the Christian faith.

⁓

I came from God. There is nothing more for me to do here. Send me back to God, from whom I came!

⁓

My voices have since told me that I did a great evil in declaring that what I had done was wrong. All that I said and revoked that Thursday, I did for fear of the fire!

Alas! Had I been in the Church prison, to which I submitted myself, and been guarded by the clergy instead of my enemies, as I was promised, this misfortune would not have come to me! Ah! I appeal to God, the Great Judge, for the great injuries done to me.

In God's name, Count, you mock me! Ransom? How you jest. You have neither the will nor the power to do so!

Ha! You take great care to put down in your trial everything that is against me, but you will not write down anything that is for me!

Joan of Arc

About Jesus Christ and the Church, I simply know they're just one thing, and we shouldn't complicate the matter.

The poor folk gladly came to me, for I did them no unkindness, but helped them as much as I could.

King of England, and you, duke of Bedford, who call yourself regent of the kingdom of France, settle your debt to the king of Heaven; return to the Maiden, who is envoy of the king of Heaven, the keys to all the good towns you took and violated in France.

Chapter 9

William Shakespeare

William Shakespeare, born on April 23, 1564, was an English poet and playwright who was called "Bard of Avon." He was considered by many to be the greatest dramatist of all time. His works consist of 38 plays, 154 sonnets, and several poems. He wrote Hamlet, King Lear, Macbeth, and Romeo & Juliet which were considered some of his finest works. William Shakespeare died on April 23, 1616. Today his plays remain very popular and are performed throughout the world.

William Shakespeare

Be not afraid of greatness; some are born great, some achieve greatness, and others have greatness thrust upon them.

All that live must die, passing through nature to eternity.

A friend is one that knows you as you are, understands where you have been, accepts what you have become, and still, gently allows you to grow.

These earthly godfathers of Heaven's lights, that give a name to every fixed star, have no more profit of their shining nights than those that walk and know not what they are.

Honestly is the best policy. If I lose mine honor, I lose myself.

Suspicion always haunts the guilty mind; the thief doth fear each bush an officer.

William Shakespeare

Love to faults is always blind, always is to joy inclined. Lawless, winged, and unconfirmed, and breaks all chains from every mind.

Words are easy, like the wind; Faithful friends are hard to find.

If you prick us do we not bleed? If you tickle us do we not laugh? If you poison us do we not die? And if you wrong us shall we not revenge?

A miser grows rich by seeming poor. An extravagant man grows poor by seeming rich.

Conversation should be pleasant without scurrility, witty without affection, free with indecency, learned without conceitedness, novel without falsehood.

That which ordinary men are fit for, I am qualified in. And the best of me is diligence.

William Shakespeare

By medicine life may be prolonged, yet death will seize the doctor too.

This is the monstrosity in love, lady, that the will is infinite and the execution is confined; that the desire is boundless, and the act a slave to limit.

That, if then I had waked after a long sleep, will make me sleep again; and then, in dreaming, the clouds me thought would open and show riches ready to drop upon me; that, when I wake I cried to dream again.

While you live tell the truth shame the devil.

It provokes the desire but it takes away the performance. Therefore much drink may be said to be an equivocator with lechery. It makes him and it mars him; it sets him on and it takes him off.

They do not love that do not show their love. The course of true love never did run smooth. Love is a familiar. Love is a devil. There is no evil angel but Love.

William Shakespeare

My crown is in my heart, not on my head. Nor decked with diamonds and Indian stones, nor to be seen. My crown is called content. A crown it is, that seldom kings enjoy.

O thou invisible spirit of wine, if thou hast no name to be known by, let us call thee devil.

The very substance of the ambitious is merely the shadow of a dream.

O curse of marriage that we can call these delicate creatures ours and not their appetites!

How sharper than a serpent's tooth it is to have a thankless child.

I told you, sir, they were red-hot with drinking; so full of valor that they smote the air, for breathing in their faces, beat the ground for kissing their feet.

William Shakespeare

Oh! It offends me to the soul to hear a robust periwig-pated fellow, tear a passion to tatters, to very rags, to split the ears of the groundlings.

Suit the action to the world, the world to the action, with this special observance, that you overstep not the modesty of nature.

I have lived long enough. My way of life is to fall into the sere, the yellow leaf, and that which should accompany old age, as honor, love, obedience, troops of friends I must not look to have.

Conceit, more rich in matter than in words, brags of his substance. They are but beggars who can count their worth.

God hath given you one face, and you make yourselves another.

When workmen strive to do better than well, they do confound their skill in covetousness.

William Shakespeare

The friends thou hast, and their adoption tried, grapple them to thy soul with hoops of steel, but do not dull thy palm with entertainment of each new-hatched unfledged comrade.

The devil can site scripture for his own purpose! An evil soul producing holy witness is like a villain with a smiling cheek.

Reputation, reputation, reputation! O, I ha lost my reputation, I ha lost the immortal part of myself, and what remains is bestial!

She's beautiful, and therefore to be wooed; She is a woman, therefore to be won.

The man that hath no music in himself, nor is not moved with concord of sweet sounds, is fit for treasons, stratagems, and spoils. The motions of his spirit are dull as night and his affections dark as Erebus. Let no such man be trusted.

The evil that men do lives after them; the good is oft interred with their bones.

Chapter 10

Mark Twain

Samuel Langhorne Clemens, better known as Mark Twain, was born on November 30, 1835. He was an American author and humorist. Twain wrote many novels and was most noted for the novels *Adventures of Huckleberry Finn* and *The Adventures of Tom Sawyer*. He wrote 28 books and numerous short stories, letters, and sketches. Mark Twain died on April 21, 1910.

Mark Twain

When your friends begin to flatter you on how young you look, it's a sure sign you're getting old.

When I was fourteen, my father was so ignorant I could hardly stand to have him around. When I got to be twenty-one, I was astonished at how much he had learned in seven years.

When I was younger, I could remember anything, whether it had happened or not.

I never could tell a lie that anybody would doubt, nor a truth that anybody would believe.

We never become really and genuinely our entire and honest selves until we are dead, and not then until we have been dead for years and years. People ought to start dead and then they would be honest so much earlier.

There are two times in a man's life when he should not speculate: when he can't afford, and when he can.

Mark Twain

Courage is resistance to fear, mastery of fear, not absence of fear.

To cease smoking is the easiest the thing I ever did, I ought to know because I've done it a thousand times.

Training is everything. The peach was once a bitter almond; cauliflower is nothing, but cabbage with a college education.

Forgiveness is the fragrance the violet sheds on the heel that has crushed it.

We owe a deep debt of gratitude to Adam, the first great benefactor of the human race; he brought death into the world.

It is better to keep your mouth closed and let people think you are a fool than to open it and remove all doubt.

Mark Twain

Thunder is impressive, but it is lightning that does the work.

The trouble with the world is not that people know to little, but that they know so many things that ain't so.

To be good is noble, but to teach others how to be good is nobler and less trouble.

If you pick a starving dog and make him prosperous, he will not bite you; that is the principle difference between a dog and a man.

In the real world, nothing happens at the right place and the right time. It is the job if journalists and historians to correct that.

It is not best that we should all think alike; it is a difference of opinion that makes horse races.

Mark Twain

War talk by men who have been in a war is always interesting; whereas moon talk by a poet who has not been in the moon is likely to be dull.

The most difficult we do not deal in facts when we are contemplating ourselves.

No God and no religion can survive ridicule. No political church, no nobility, no royalty or other fraud, can face ridicule in a fair field, and live.

Scientists have odious manners; except when you prop up their theory; then you can borrow money of them.

Wrinkles should merely indicate where smiles have been.

Forget and forgive. This is not difficult when properly understood. It means forget inconvenient duties, then forgive yourself for forgetting. By rigid practice and stern determination, it comes easy.

Mark Twain

It is better to deserve honors and not have them than to have them and not deserve them.

Public opinion is held in reverence. It settles everything. Some think it is the voice of God.

Life would be infinitely happier if we could only be born at the age of eighty and gradually approach eighteen.

The human race was always interesting and we know by its past that it will always continue so, monotonously.

You cannot depend on your judgments when your imagination is our of focus.

Fortune knocks at every man's door once in a life, but in a good many cases the man is in a neighboring salon and does not hear her.

Mark Twain

It ain't those parts of the Bible that I can't understand that bother me, it is the parts I do understand.

Keep away from small people who try to belittle your ambitions. Small people always do that, but the really great make you feel that you, too, can become great.

I can teach anybody how to get what they want out of life. The problem is that I can't find anybody who can tell me what they want.

Chapter 11

Robert Frost

Robert Frost, born on March 26, 1874, was an American poet. Through his work, he frequently associated with the life and landscape of New England. Frost had many published collections. Some of his works include *A Boy's Will*, *North of Boston*, *New Hampshire*, *A Further Range*, *Steeple Bush*, and *In the Clearing*. Frost received many honors in his life and four Pulitzer Prizes for poetry. Robert Frost died on January 29, 1963.

Robert Frost

The brain is a wonderful organ; it starts working the moment you get up in the morning and does not stop until you get to the office.

A champion of the working man has never yet been known to die of overwork.

We dance around in a ring and suppose, but the secret sits in the middle and knows.

Poetry is what is lost in translation.

Always fall in with what you're asked to accept. Take what is given, and make it over your way. My aim in life has always been to hold my own with whatever's going. Not against; with.

Two roads diverge in a wood, and I took the one less traveled by, and that has made all the difference.

Robert Frost

I often say of George Washington that he was one of the few in the whole history of the world who has not carried away by power.

But I have promises to keep, and miles to go before I sleep, and miles to go before I sleep.

The reason why worry kills more people than work is that more people worry than work.

The greatest thing in family life is to take a hint when a hint is intended; and not to take a hint when a hint isn't intended.

The world is full of willing people, some willing to work, the rest willing to let them.

An idea is a feat of association, and the height of it is a good metaphor.

Robert Frost

Most of the change we think we see in life is due to truths being in and out of favor.

There is little much beyond the grave, but the strong are saying nothing until they see.

In three words I can sum up everything I've learned about life. It goes on.

By working faithfully eight hours a day, you may eventually get to be a boss and work twelve hours a day.

You don't have to deserve your mother's love. You have to deserve your father s. He's more particular. The father is always a Republican towards his son, and his mother's always a Democrat.

I never dared to be radical when young for fear it would make me conservative when old.

Robert Frost

Forgive, O Lord, my little jokes on Thee and I'll forgive Thy great big one on me.

Heaven gives us glimpses only to those not in position to look too close.

I would as soon write free verse as play tennis with the net down.

You can be a little ungrammatical if you come from the right part of the country.

A poem begins as a lump in the throat, a sense of wrong, a homesickness, a lovesickness. It finds the thought and the thought finds the words.

A diplomat is a man who always remembers a woman's birthday but never remembers her age.

Robert Frost

"Skepticism," is that anything more than we used to mean when we said, "Well, what have we here?"

Don't ever take a fence down until you know why it was put up.

There is the fear that we shan't prove worthy in the eyes of someone who knows us at least as well as we know ourselves. That is the fear of God. And there is the fear of Man, fear that men won't understand us and we shall be cut of from them.

Time and tide wait for no man, but time always stands still for a woman of 30.

A liberal man is too broad-minded to take his own side in a quarrel.

A mother takes twenty years to make a man of her boy, and another woman makes a fool of him in twenty minutes.

Chapter 12

Mother Teresa

Mother Teresa, born on August 26, 1910, was an Albanian Catholic nun with Indian citizenship. In 1950, she founded the Missionnaries of Charity in Calcutta, India which operates today in over 100 cities worldwide. She was a great humanitarian and advocate for the poor, sick, and dying. In 1979 Mother Teresa was awarded the Nobel Peace Prize and the Bharat Ratna in 1980 for her humanitarian work. Mother Teresa died on September 5, 1997.

Mother Teresa

Even the rich are hungry for love, for being cared for, for being wanted, for having someone to call their own.

If you want a love message to be heard, it has got to be sent out. To keep a lamp burning, we have to keep putting oil in it.

Kind words can be short and easy to speak, but their echoes are truly endless.

Do not wait for leaders; do it alone, person to person.

Every time you smile at someone, it is an action of love, a gift to that person, a beautiful thing.

The miracle is not that we do this work, but that we are happy to do it.

Mother Teresa

There are no great things, only small things with great love. Happy are those.

We need to find God, and he cannot be found in noise and restlessness. God is the friend of silence. See how nature—trees, flowers, grass-grows in silence; see the stars, the moon and the sun, how they move in silence. We need silence to be able to touch souls.

Being unwanted, unloved, uncared for, forgotten by everybody, I think that is a much greater hunger, a much greater poverty than the person who has nothing to eat.

I have found the paradox, that if you love until it hurts, there can be no more hurt, only more love.

If you judge people, you have no time to love them.

Sweetest Lord, make me appreciative of the dignity of my high vocation, and its many responsibilities. Never permit me to disgrace it by giving way to coldness, unkindness, or impatience.

Mother Teresa

There is always the danger that we may just do the work for the sake of the work. This is where the respect and the love and the devotion come in—that we do it to God, to Christ, and that's why we try to do it as beautifully as possible.

I am a little pencil in the hand of a writing God who is sending a love letter to the world.

I want you to be concerned about your next door neighbor. Do you know your next door neighbor?

We ourselves feel that what we are doing is just a drop in the ocean. But the ocean would be less because of that missing drop.

I know that God will not give me anything I can't handle. I just wish that He didn't trust me so much.

If you can't feed a hundred people, then feed just one.

Mother Teresa

I try to give to the poor people for love what the rich could get for money. No, I wouldn't touch a leper for a thousand pounds; yet I willingly cure him for the love of God.

It is a poverty to decide that a child must die so that you may live as you wish.

Jesus said love one another. He didn't say love the whole world.

Let us not be satisfied with just giving money. Money is not enough, money can be got, but they need your hearts to love them. So, spread your love everywhere you go.

Love begins by taking care of the closest ones, the ones at home.

Words which do not give the light of Christ increase the darkness.

Mother Teresa

The greatest destroyer of peace is abortion because if a mother can kill her own child, what is left for me to kill you and you to kill me? There is nothing between.

There is more hunger in the world for love and appreciation in this world than for bread.

We, the unwilling, led by the unknowing, are doing the impossible for the ungrateful. We have done so much, for so long, with so little, we are now qualified to do anything with nothing.

The biggest disease today is not leprosy or tuberculosis, but rather the feeling of being unwanted.

There must be a reason why some people can afford to live well. They must have worked for it. I only feel angry when I see waste. When I see people throwing away things that we could use.

It is not the magnitude of our actions but the amount of love that is put into them that matters.

Chapter 13

7 Steps to Longevity

1. Change your Attitude

When you wake up out of bed, smile and say, "Today is going to be a good day and I feel great!" Your thoughts and words are very powerful. Positive thinking and optimism can lead you to a healthier and happier lifestyle. Positive thinking should be practiced daily to create a positive attitude. When you have a positive attitude, you are creating a positive environment, and in return, you are manifesting a successful and fulfilling life.

2. Eat Healthy

You have heard the phrase, "Your body is like an engine, and food is the fuel it needs to keep it going." Well, this is very true. If we do not eat a healthy diet, our bodies can become weak, sick, or even death can occur. It is imperative to eat a variety of foods to receive the proper nutrients and minerals that the body needs to function. Every fruit and vegetable has a nutritional benefit to promote good health and energy for the body. Protein is a major component of all muscles, tissues, and organs and is vital for the growth, maintenance, and repair of all cells. It is important to eat a variety of grains, which provide many nutrients, including dietary fiber, several vitamins and minerals for our bodies. Milk and dairy products provide calcium, which is essential for healthy bones. And, of course, staying hydrated is very crucial to our health. Your body is composed of 60% water—the most important nutrient you can give to the body.

3. Set Goals

Before you begin your day, think about what you would like to accomplish or plan for the day. Giving yourself a sense of direction will give you confidence, a purpose, and help you reach your goals. It doesn't matter if your goal is big or small. You decide what is important to you and how you want to get there. We are sometimes faced with fear and obstacles, which makes it harder to reach our goals. Whatever your mission may be, having motivation and a clear, positive mindset will attract success. Keep in mind, you may not achieve your goal, but consider life may have another purpose for you.

4. Exercise

Exercise plays an important role in maintaining a healthy body and improving the quality of life. Experts recommend that you do at least two hours and thirty minutes a week of moderate aerobic activity or one hour and fifteen minutes a week of vigorous aerobic activity—preferably spread throughout the week. Strength training exercises are recommended at least twice a week. Stretching is a good warmup for the body. Stretching increases flexibility, improves circulation, range of motion, and reduces stress. However, overstretching—stretching to the point where we feel pain, may make our joints more unstable and prone to injury.

Here are some key benefits from exercising:

- Decreased Heart Attack
- Decreased the Risk of Cancers
- Increased Stamina
- Reduced Depression
- Reduced Stress Levels
- Increased Energy
- Manage Weight

5. Massage

Massage is thought to be one of the oldest healing arts dating back 3,000 years in Chinese records. The ancient Egyptians, Persians, and Hindus used massage to preserve health and treat various aliments. Today we use massage which is known to be a healing technique for the body, mind, and spirit. Massage has been scientifically proven to have beneficial results for many chronic conditions. It increases longevity, productivity, circulation, sensation, mobility, and relaxation. Massage is not recommended if you suffer from a fever, high blood pressure, varicose veins, inflammation, hernia, infectious diseases, cancers, or skin problems. Consider a massage at least once a month to remove toxins and reduce the stress levels in the body. Beneficial for babies, children, adults, and the elderly, massage is a service used in hospitals, health care centers, clinics, and spas.

6. Meditate

Life can be very chaotic and stressful at times, giving us limited time to examine or reflect. When there is no noise, just silence, our mind becomes more focused, we are calm, and we are less stressed. Meditation is a way for us to bring balance and harmony in our lives, giving us an inner peace. Through meditation, we can channel a higher consciousness and increase our intuition. Meditation has been proven to have many psychological, physical, and spiritual benefits. Set aside a time for meditation every day. A good start is about ten to fifteen minutes a day, anytime of the day. Later you may decide to increase your meditation time. Buddha's quote: "Meditation brings wisdom; lack of meditation brings ignorance. Know well what leads you forward and what holds you back, and choose the path that leads to wisdom."

7. Sleep

Sleep is essential for our mental and physical health. When we do not get the proper rest needed for our bodies, we can become very restless, moody, and unable to function properly during the day. When we sleep, the body heals itself, repairing damage caused by stress and removing toxins from the body. A "power nap" has been proven to be very effective—improving memory, cognitive function and mood. Sleeping a minimum of six to eight hours per night plays a vital role in our overall well-being. Experts say that sleeping less than six hours a night or sleeping too much may cause serious health problems. If you have trouble falling asleep, here are a few techniques you may want to try:

- Talk to a physician
- Listen to relaxing music
- Take a warm bath
- Avoid caffeine
- Drink warm milk
- Drink herbal tea

"Mother Earth"

Weeping alone, no ear atones, I bow humbly in despair. Forgiving the hand that unleashed the pain that only I know so well. "Why?" I ask while weeping floods of tears... "does my pain fall on deaf ears?"
I give you life... I give you beauty... I give you paradise. I made a promise—though it goes unheard—my mere existence for you I would sacrifice.
So heed my warning... for now I shout with floods, earthquakes, famine and death; since it is I you spit upon with no apt of regret. Again, for you I shed my tears and speak the words of truth... It is not I who will cease to live... but YOU; and that is a fact! Mother Earth is who I am; I say it loud and clear! Mother Earth is who I am; and I will take it back!

By Shirley R Hooper
(my mother)

Other Recommended Books

Feeling Good: The new mood therapy, by David D. Burns

The 7 Habits of Highly Effective People: " How to be truly effective and organized", by Stephen R. Covey

The Courage to be Yourself: A woman's guide to emotional strength and self-esteem, by Sue Patton Thoele

Spiritual Growth: Being your higher self, by Sanaya Roman

The Power of Now: A guide to spiritual enlightenment, by Eckhart Tolle

The Secrets of the Light: Spiritual Strategies to Empower Your Life... Here and in the Hereafter, by Dannion Brinkley

And one of my personal favorites:

Embraced by the Light: by Betty J. Eadie

Other Recommended Audios

Fearless Love: The answer to the problem of human existence, by Gary Renard

The Power of the Soul: The way to heal, rejuvenate, transform and enlighten all life, by Zhi Gang Sha

The UltraMind Solution: Fix your broken brain by healing your body first, by Mark, M.D. Hyman

Your Present: A half hour of peace, by Susie Mantell

Psychic Navigator: Harnessing your inner guidance, by John Holland

Conversations with God: by Neale Donald Walsch

www.ingramcontent.com/pod-product-compliance
Lightning Source LLC
Chambersburg PA
CBHW061655040426
42446CB00010B/1747